Beaver State Confidential
A Citizen's Guide to Oregon State Government

Alex McHaddad

Copyright Alex McHaddad, 2022. All rights reserved

No part of this book may be reproduced, or stored in a retrieval system, or transmitted in any form or by any means, electronic, mechanical, photocopying, recording, or otherwise, without express written permission of the publisher.

ISBN-13: 979-8-9856444-3-2
Library of Congress Control Number: 2022921321

Works By Alex McHaddad

Beaver State Confidential

Sands of Jannah: Ignoble

Learn More

www.alexfor.us

Table of Contents

Introduction..5

Chapter 1: The Executive Branch..6

Chapter 2: The Legislature...34

Chapter 3: The Capitol..42

Chapter 4: Courts & Public Safety..51

Chapter 6: Education..71

Chapter 7: Oregon Culture...80

Chapter 8: How a Bill Becomes Law.....................................89

Epilogue: Leading in Oregon..100

Introduction

Beaver State Confidential is a manual for understanding how the greatest state in the Union is governed. Any reader, whether a citizen hoping to improve their civic awareness or a candidate for Governor, can pick up this manual and quickly learn about how a bill becomes law, the duties of different government officials, and the wide range of opportunities to shape public policy.

After years of advocating in Salem, managing local government agencies, serving on appointed boards, leading political parties, and reporting Oregon news, I'm excited to share my love for Oregon with fellow Beaver State residents. While I have my own opinions and beliefs shaped by my experiences in the Capitol and throughout the state, I'm proud to share the unbiased basics of state government with all readers. Any insights that come from personal experience rather than a cited source will be noted.

Grab a copy, sit down with your favorite IPA, and learn about Oregon's history, government, and culture. You're about to become an expert on the Beaver State!

Chapter 1: The Executive Branch

European exploration of what was known as the Oregon Country began in the 1700's. Land and sea expeditions from the British Empire and the United States began exploring what would become Oregon, Washington, Idaho, and British Columbia. The first true authority figure in the Oregon Country was John McLoughlin, who served as Chief Factor of the Columbia District for Hudson's Bay Company. His leadership of the region began in 1824 and extended through 1845.

Image: John McLoughlin Monument, Oregon State Capitol.

As settlers from the United States began forming their own government in the 1800's to begin the process of statehood, Dr. McLoughlin advanced to retirement. Settlers gathered to discuss local governance at the small community of Champoeg on the Willamette River north of modern-day Salem in 1841.

Images: Champoeg State Park.

The first day of meetings was chaired by circuit-riding preacher Jason Lee, who could be considered the first popularly-elected leader of Oregon. The second day, meetings were chaired by David Leslie. Settlers chose Dr. Ira Babcock to serve as the first and only Supreme Judge of the Oregon Country, a position he held for two years. Judge Babcock promised to govern using the Statutes from New York State - though it was hidden from settlers that he did not in fact have a copy of these statutes, and he governed and judged as he pleased.

Image: Reverend Jason Lee Monument, Oregon State Capitol.

After Ira Babock's tenure ended in 1843, settlers created the Provisional Government. This body was governed by a three-member executive committee for two terms. After this, the Oregon Country was governed by the first person to hold the title of Governor, George Abernathy, who served a pair of two-year terms from 1845-1849.

The Oregon and Washington Territories were officially created by the United States Congress in 1848. Provisional Governors were appointed by Presidents of the United States and approved by Congress until 1859, when Oregon was admitted to the Union.

37 individuals have served as Governor of Oregon since 1859, starting with John Whiteaker and leading to Kate Brown. Several individuals have become Governor as the result of a vacancy in the office due to federal appointment, death, and resignation.

Oath of Office

I, [Name], do solemnly swear [or affirm], that I will support the Constitution of the United States, and the Constitution of the State of Oregon, and that I will faithfully discharge the duties of Governor according to the best of my ability.

Demographics: Governors of the State of Oregon

Governors: 37
Women: 2
Openly LGBT: 1
Died In Office: 4
Born Overseas: 4
Living Former Governors: 4
Served In Congress: 7
Served AS Diplomats: 2

Served In The US Cabinet: 2
Served As Governor Of Another Territory: 1
Born In Oregon: 10
Democrats: 17
Republicans: 20
Non-affiliated: 1

Hudson's Bay Company
- Columbia District Chief Factor John McLoughlin, 1824-1845.

Champoeg Meetings
- Chair Jason Lee. February 17, 1841.
- Chair David Leslie. February 18, 1841.
- Supreme Judge Ira Babcock. February 18, 1841-May 2, 1843.

Provisional Government
- First Executive Committee, July 5 1843-May 14, 1844
- Second Executive Committee, May 14, 1844-June 3, 1845
- Governor George Abernathy, June 3, 1845-March 3, 1849

Territorial Governors

- Joseph Lane (Democrat). March 3, 1849-June 18, 1850.
- Kintzing Prichette (Democrat). June 18, 1850-August 18, 1850 (Acting Governor).
- John Gaines (Whig). August 18, 1850-May 16, 8153.
- Joseph Lane (Democrat). May 16, 1853-May 19, 1853 (Acting Governor).
- George Curry (Democrat). May 19, 1853-December 2, 1853 (Acting Governor).
- John Davis (Democrat). December 2, 1853-August 1, 1854.
- George Curry (Democrat). August 1, 1854-March 3, 1859.

State Governors

- John Whiteaker (Democrat). March 3, 1859-September 10, 1862. Not nominated in 1862 Democratic Primary.
- A.C. Gibbs (Republican). September 10, 1862-September 12, 1866. Unsuccessfully ran for US Senate.
- George Woods (Republican). September 12, 1866- September 14, 1870. Lost re-election; appointed Territorial Governor of Utah.
- La Fayette Grover (Democrat). September 14, 1870-February 1, 1877. Elected to U.S. Senate.
- Stephen Chadwick (Democrat). February 1, 1877-September 11, 1878. Did not seek re-election.
- W.W. Thayer (Democrat). September 11, 1878-September 13, 1882. Did not seek re-election.
- Zenas Moody (Republican). September 13, 1882-January 12, 1887.
- Sylvester Pennoyer (Democrat). January 12, 1887-January 14, 1895. First Governor to serve two terms (term-limited).
- William Lord (Republican). January 14, 1895-January 9, 1899. Lost re-election.
- Theodore Geer (Republican). January 9, 1899-January 15, 1903.
- George Chamberlain (Democrat). January 15, 1903-March 1, 1909. Elected to U.S. Senate.

- Frank Benson (Republican). March 1, 1909-June 17, 1910. Ceded authority to Acting Governor.
- Jay Bowerman (Republican). June 17, 1910-January 11, 1911. Acting Governor; lost election to a full term.
- Oswald West (Democrat). January 11, 1911-January 12, 1915. Did not seek re-election.
- James Withycombe (Republican). January 12, 1915-March 3, 1919. First Governor to die in office.
- Ben Olcott (Republican). March 3, 1919-January 8, 1923. Lost re-election.
- Walter Pierce (Democrat). January 8, 1923-January 10, 1927. Did not win re-election.
- I.L. Patterson (Republican). January 10, 1927-December 21, 1929. Died in office.
- A.W. Norblad (Republican). December 21, 1929-January 12, 1931. Not nominated in 1930 Republican Primary.
- Julius Meier (Non-affiliated). January 12, 1931-January 14, 1935. Did not seek re-election.
- Charles Martin (Democrat). January 14, 1935-January 9, 1939. Not nominated in 1938 election.
- Charles Sprague (Republican). January 9, 1939-January 11, 1943. Not nominated in 1942 election.
- Earl Snell (Republican). January 11, 1943-

October 30, 1947. Died while in office in plane crash along with the Secretary of State and Senate President.
- John Hall (Republican). October 30, 1947-January 10, 1949. Not nominated in 1948 election.
- Douglas McKay (Republican). January 10, 1949-December 27, 1952. Appointed U.S. Secretary of the Interior.
- Paul Patterson (Republican). December 27, 1952-February 1, 1956. Died in office.
- Elmo Smith (Republican). February 1, 1956-January 14, 1957. Lost re-election.
- Robert Holmes (Democrat). January 14, 1957-January 12, 1959. Lost re-election.
- Mark Hatfield (Republican). January 12, 1959-January 9, 1967. Term-limited; elected to U.S. Senate.
- Tom McCall (Republican). January 9, 1967-January 13, 1975. Term-limited.
- Robert Straub (Democrat). January 13, 1975-January 8, 1979. Lost re-election.
- Victor Atiyeh (Republican). January 8, 1979-January 12, 1987. Term-limited.
- Neil Goldschmidt (Democrat). January 12, 1987-January 14, 1991. Did not seek re-election.
- Barbara Roberts (Democrat). January 14, 1991-January 9, 1995. Did not seek re-election.

- John Kitzhaber (Democrat). January 9, 1995-January 13, 2003. Term-limited.
- Ted Kulongoski (Democrat). January 13, 2003-January 10, 2011. Term-limited.
- John Kitzhaber (Democrat). January 10, 2011-February 18, 2015. Resigned.
- Kate Brown (Democrat). February 18, 2015-present. Incumbent.

Image: Portrait of Governor John Kitzhaber in the Oregon Capitol, photo taken the day before his resignation.

Tenure

John Kitzhaber of Portland served the longest time in office, elected four terms before resigning one month into his fourth term as he dealt with an ethics investigation. Elmo Smith of Ontario served less than one year in office following the death of his predecessor, Paul Patterson. Nine Governors succeeded to the office due to a vacancy in the position. Only six Governors have served two full terms.

Lieutenant Governors

In many states, the Governor is elected alongside a Lieutenant Governor, just as the U.S. President is elected alongside a Vice President. The Lieutenant Governor is usually the presiding officer of their respective state's senate, and is always first in line to fill vacancies in the office of Governor. Oregon has no Lieutenant Governor.

Gubernatorial Succession

Gubernatorial vacancies are filled in order by the Secretary of State, Treasurer, President of the Senate, and Speaker of the House.

The Governor's Mansion: Mahonia Hall

Oregon did not designate an official Governor's mansion until 1988. Mahonia Hall is named after the scientific name of Oregon's State flower, mahonia aquifolium, the first place in a naming contest sponsored by The Oregonian newspaper. Governor Neil Goldschmidt was the first to occupy Mahonia Hall. Governor John Kitzhaber did not use Mahonia Hall as a resident, but it was utilized by Governors Barbara Roberts, Ted Kulongoski, and Kate Brown.

Governor's Office

The Governor of Oregon has offices in the Oregon State Capitol, the structure in Salem that houses the Legislative Assembly and other important executive branch officials. Governors have business offices where staff perform work under the direction of the Governor's Chief of Staff. A ceremonial office is maintained in the Capitol where state relics are on display, including a small Oregon flag that was present during a moon landing. The Governor conducts public bill signings and holds press conferences in this office.

Powers of the Governor

The powers of the Governor are enumerated in Article V of the Oregon Constitution:
- Act as chief executive of the government (Section 1).
- Serve as commander in chief of state military forces (Section 9).
- Execute state laws (Section 10).
- Recommend legislation (Section 11).
- Convene the Legislative Assembly (Section 12).
- Transact all government business, and require information from state officials (Section 13).
- Grant pardons and commute sentences (Section 14).
- Veto legislation, veto single items in appropriation bills, and veto emergency declarations in bills (Section 15a).
- Sign legislation, or request amendments before signing (Section 15b).
- Appoint agency executives, agency board members, and interstate board members, as well as fill vacancies in certain locally elected offices (Section 16).
- Issue writs of election to fill vacancies in the Legislative Assembly (17).

The Governor's Staff

The Governor is assisted by a large workforce of staff in Salem and across the state. Staff specialize in several and administrative policy arenas.

- Addictions & Recovery/Opioid Epidemic/Oregon Liquor Control Commission/Gaming
- Administration/
- Scheduling
- Executive Appointments
- Federal Affairs
- General Counsel
- Health
- Housing
- Human Services
- Jobs and Economy
- Labor
- Legislative
- Natural Resources
- Climate, Energy and Transportation
- Communications
- Constituent Services
- Education
- Equity and Racial Justice Office
- Operations
- Public Records
- Public Safety/Military
- Regional Solutions
- Resilience
- Tribal Affairs
- Veterans
- Wildfire
- Wildfire Recovery
- Workforce

State Agencies

The Governor has authority over all state agencies not under the jurisdiction of other statewide elected officials or the Legislative Assembly. Many state agencies are led by a board or commission appointed by the Governor, with these bodies empowered to appoint the agency's chief executive. Other agency heads have a director appointed by the Governor, and may or may not have an associated commission. The Governor is the ex officio Superintendent of Public Instruction, overseeing the Oregon Department of Education.

Department of Administrative Services

Oregon's most powerful executive state agency is the Department of Administrative Services (DAS). The responsibilities assigned to DAS include implementing policy and financial decisions made by the Governor and Legislative Assembly, coordinating projects involving multiple state agencies, and catalyzing innovation and improvement in state government. The Director of DAS, Katy Coba, also carries the title of Chief Operating Officer of the state government.

Agency Chief Executive Appointments

The Governor directly appoints the heads of several state agencies, including the following:

- Department of Administrative Services
- Department of Agriculture
- Department of Aviation
- Department of Business Development
- Department of Employment
- Department of Energy
- State Fire Marshal
- State Geologist
- Department of Housing & Community Services
- Department of Human Services
- Department of Land Conservation and Development
- Military Department
- Department of Parks & Recreation
- Department of Consumer & Business Services
- Department of Corrections
- Deputy Superintendent of Public Instruction
- Department of Public Safety Standards & Training
- Department of Revenue
- Department of State Lands
- State Policy Superintendent
- Department of Transportation
- Department of Veterans Affairs
- Department of Water Resources

Board and Commission Appointments

The Governor appoints members of over 300 boards and task forces, though only over 100 of them require the Senate confirmation. Some of the bodies appointed by the Governor requiring Senate confirmation include the following:

- Alcohol & Drug Policy Commission
  Apprenticeship & Training Council
  Commission on Asian & Pacific Islander Affairs
  Commission on Black Affairs
  Board of Boiler Rules
  Building Codes Structures Board
- Fish & Wildlife Commission
- Government Ethics Commission
- Oregon Health & Science University Board of Directors
- Health Evidence Review Commission
- Health Insurance Exchange Advisory Committee

Public Addresses

The Governor is tasked with informing the public about important federal, state, and local government information. Governors will use public addresses or press releases to communicate important updates. They also use public addresses to advocate for policies or discuss the work they have performed on behalf of their constituents.

Governor Kate Brown, 10/1/2015
Governor Brown Orders Flags Lowered to Half-Staff for Umpqua Community College Shooting: *Governor Kate Brown immediately orders flags lowered to half-staff at all public institutions throughout Oregon until sunset on Friday, Oct. 2 in honor of the victims of the Umpqua Community College shooting.*

"Today is heartbreaking for Umpqua Community College, the greater Roseburg community, and all of Oregon," Governor Brown said. "My heart is heavy as we continue to learn more about today's tragic events. While it is still too early to know all of the facts, the effects of an incident such as this one are long-lasting. Please join me in keeping the victims and their families, as well as first responders, in your thoughts."

Following her press conference on the shooting this afternoon, Governor Brown is en route to Roseburg.

Governor John Kitzhaber, 9/11/01

Governor's Statement On Terrorist Attacks: *This is a tragic day for the nation.*

The horrible events unfolding in New York City and in the nation's capital are incomprehensible. Our hearts and prayers go out to the victims of this savage and unthinkable attack on America.

It is a time of shock and sorrow. It is also a time for calm and courage.

Let me first reassure Oregonians we have no intelligence from either federal or state sources suggesting any threat to our state or any Oregonian.

However, we will take every reasonable precaution to assure our safety. We have instituted a heightened level of security. Federal buildings and the Bonneville Power Administration offices have been closed.

And clearly, the Portland International Airport has been closed at the direction of the Federal Aviation Administration. Again, these are precautionary actions, not based on any intelligence reports of a threat.

Around the state, I have asked all state offices to remain open. The Oregon Capitol Building will remain open.

Fellow Oregonians, I urge you all to remain calm. There is no need for panic. From everything we know, Oregon is not at risk. Take a deep breath; find the courage to go on with your day, and focus your thoughts and prayers on the victims of these attacks and their families.

Executive Orders

The Governor issues Executive Orders to implement state law. Executive Orders are drafted by legal counsel in the Governor's Office to ensure that laws are properly enforced as the results of these documents. Some are complex, creating new state bodies as required by the Legislative Assembly. Others are more complex. Governor Kate Brown issued Executive Order 19-03 in 2019 to create the Child Welfare Oversight Board, amended later via Executive Order 19-07.

Executive Order No. 19-07: Amending Executive Order No. 1903

Executive Order 19-03 was issued on April 18, 2019. On page 3 of Executive Order 19-03, Section 3 is amended to provide as follows:
This Executive Order shall be effective until December 31, 2019, at which time it shall expire unless extended by the Governor.
Done at Salem, Oregon, this 26th day of September, 2019.
Kate Brown, GOVERNOR
Attest: Bev Clarno, SECRETARY OF STATE

Executive Clemencies

Oregon's Constitution empowers the Governor to grant reprieves, commutations, and pardons for all offenses except treason. The Governor may refer individuals convicted of treason to the Legislative Assembly to consider clemency. Executive clemencies are regularly reported to the Legislative Assembly under state law.

June 2019 Executive Summary of Executive Clemencies

TO: Members of the Legislative Assembly,
FROM: Misha Isaak, General Counsel, Office of the Governor
CC: Daron M. Hill, Legislative Administrator
RE: Executive Summary of Executive Clemencies
Date: June 28, 2019

On June 28, 2019, pursuant to ORS 144.660, Governor Kate Brown transmitted a report to Senate President Courtney and Speaker Kotek outlining each reprieve, commutation, pardon, remission of penalty or forfeiture that her office processed pursuant to her constitutional authority under Article V, Section 14, of the Oregon Constitution, since the previous report to the Legislative Assembly.

Governor Kate Brown has granted six pardons and three conditional commutations. No reprieves or remissions of penalty or forfeiture have been granted. Between March 3, 2018 and today, 151 applications for commutation of sentence have been denied and one commutation applicant is deceased. There are 60 commutation applications pending. 77 pardon applications have been denied, 52 pardon applications are pending, and one pardon application was withdrawn. Two reprieve applications are pending. No remission applications are pending.

A copy of the report was provided to Legislative Administrator, Daron M. Hill, and is available from his office upon request, or from the Governor's Executive Clemency Coordinator Fran Lushenko, who can be reached via email at frances.lushenko@oregon.gov.

Please note that six applicants have applied for more than one type of executive clemency. This report accounts for each type of clemency requested as a separate application.

September 2021 Commutation Denial

Dear [Defendant Name Not Reprinted],

I have received and reviewed your application for a commutation of sentence.

The power to grant executive clemency is a responsibility that I take very seriously. I believe that Governor's clemency power should be exercised sparingly. The separation of powers inherent in our system of government and respect for the workings of the judicial system require that the Governor's clemency power be used in only the most extraordinary of circumstances.

I have considered carefully whether your application for commutation should be granted. Under the circumstances, I have concluded that a commutation is not warranted. I am therefore denying your application.

Sincerely,

Governor Kate Brown

Secretary of State

The Secretary of State is the second most powerful statewide elected official, charged with a wide array of duties under the Constitution including managing elections, auditing state agencies, and maintaining records of state and corporate affairs. The Provisional and Territory governments of Oregon each had five Secretaries of State, followed by 28 since Statehood. Due to the close line of succession to the Governor's office, several Secretaries of State have succeeded to that office due to a vacancy, or were elected to higher positions later.

Territorial and State Governors Kintzing Prichette, George Curry, Stephen Chadwick, Frank Benson, Ben Olcott, Earl Snell, Mark Hatfield, Tom McCall, Barbara Roberts, and Kate Brown all served as Secretary of State.

Following Kate Brown's succession to the Governorship, Jeanne Atkins was appointed to the position and later served as Chair of the Democratic Party of Oregon. The late Dennis Richardson was replaced by former House Speaker Bev Clarno following his death in office.

The Secretary of State's office is located on the first floor of the Oregon State Capitol. The Secretary of State in 2022 is Democrat Shemia Fagan of Portland, a former State Senator and Representative.

State Treasurer

The State Treasurer has the most vaguely defined powers of the three statewide offices enumerated in the Oregon Constitution. According to the Constitution, "The powers, and duties of the Treasurer of State shall be such as may be prescribed by law." Currently, the Legislative Assembly prescribes the duties of overseeing state finances, managing billions of taxpayer dollars, investing state funds, sitting on several finance boards, and serving as the central bank for state agencies.

The Provisional Government elected six Treasurers, and the Territorial Government elected five, though Treasurer John Boon served two nonconsecutive terms. Boon was the first elected State Treasurer and the only statewide Territorial elected official to be elected to a statewide office after Oregon acceded to the Union. Thomas Kay is the longest-serving Treasurer, having filled four terms.

Few Treasurers have gone on to hold more prominent offices despite the office's proximity to power. Robert Straub is the only Treasurer to be elected Governor. Phil Metschan was an emergency replacement Republican nominee for Governor in 1930 following the death of the candidate who had won the primary. James Redden served one term before holding one elected term as Attorney General and then serving on the United States District Court for Oregon from 1980 until his death in 2020. Ted Wheeler was elected Mayor of Portland.

Left: Secretary of State's Office. Right: State Treasurer's Office

State Lands Board

Oregon's Governor, Secretary of State, and State Treasurer are constitutionally obligated to serve on the State Land Board, which governs the Department of State Lands. Upon accession to the Union, Oregon received millions of acres of land from the federal government to monetize for the purpose of funding education. The State Land Board ensures that this property is used to fund education, and fulfills additional responsibilities from the Legislative Assembly including wetland conservation and protection of public rights to use state-owned waterways.

Attorney General

The Oregon Legislative Assembly created the office of Attorney General in 1891 before reforming it in 1947. Oregon's Attorney General is the chief executive of the Department of Justice, charged with enforcing state law, defending the state in court, and providing legal guidance for state and local agencies.

17 Oregonians have served as Attorney General since 1891, including the third longest-serving statewide elected executive branch official in Oregon history, Isaac Van Winkle. Van Winkle died in 1943 during his 23rd year serving in the office. Vacancies in the office of Attorney General have only occurred five times. Ted Kulongoski went on to serve as a state Supreme Court Justice, Governor, and Western Oregon University Trustee after launching his political career in the House, the only Oregon politician to serve in all three branches of government.

The Attorney General in 2022 is Ellen Rosenblum, first appointed to the office in 2012 following the resignation of John Kroger and elected every election since 2012. Rosenblum previously served as an Assistant US Attorney, Multnomah County District Court Judge, Multnomah County Circuit Court Judge, and State Court of Appeals Judge.

BOLI Commissioner

The Oregon Legislative Assembly created the office of Oregon Labor Commission in 1903, after which the title underwent several revisions. Since 1979, the position has been entitled Oregon Commissioner of Labor & Industries, serving as the chief executive of the Bureau of Labor & Industries. Commissioners serve the longest average time in the office of all statewide elected officials, as the Legislative Assembly has never adopted term limits. Commissioner Charles Gram served in the office for 24 years, the longest tenure in a single statewide executive office in state history.

2022 Statewide Elected Officials

- Governor: Kate Brown (Democrat) of Portland.
- Secretary of State: Shemia Fagan (Democrat) of Portland.
- State Treasurer: Tobias Read (Democrat) of Portland.
- Attorney General: Ellen Rosenblum (Democrat) of Portland.
- BOLI Commissioner: Val Hoyle (Nonpartisan Office) of Eugene.

Chapter 2: The Legislature

Since the first meetings at Champoeg, Oregonians have chosen representatives to make laws promoting the general welfare and protecting essential liberties. Provisional Government laws were written by the Legislative Committee from 1843-1844 until they were replaced by the House of Representatives. The Territorial Government's lawmaking powers were passed to an elected legislature in 1849 consisting of the Council and House of Representatives. The Oregon Legislative Assembly was established upon Oregon's accession to the Union in 1859 consisting of the House of Representatives and the Senate Oregon's legislature meets in the State Capitol, where the Governor, Secretary of State, and State Treasurer also work.

The Legislative Assembly is one of the three branches of Oregon government, alongside the Executive Branch led by Oregon's 5 statewide elected officials, and the Judicial Branch.

Image: Oregon Capitol Mall.

The author first learned the details of Oregon's legislative process in 2014 during a political science course at Eastern Oregon University. Senator Bill Hansell, who represents Senate District 29, visited the class and used his experiences in the legislature to discuss the process of a bill becoming law. Passage of a law requires three key numbers: 31, 16, and 1. Bills must pass each chamber with at least a majority of all members, not just members present, which means 31 out of 60 Representatives and 16 out of 30 Senators. The Governor signs and vetoes legislation, with additional maneuvers prescribed under the Constitution.

The Senate

Modeled after the United States Congress, Oregon and all other states except Nebraska have a bicameral legislature, meaning that the body is divided into two chambers. All state upper legislative chambers are named the Senate, just like the upper chamber of Congress. Unlike the US Senate, the Oregon Senate is organized by dividing the State into 30 areas of equal population rather than a territorial basis. Under the Constitution, Oregon may have between 16-30 Senators. Expansion of the number of Senators requires voters to approve an amendment to the Constitution.

While most states elect a Lieutenant Governor to serve as the presiding officer of the Senate, members of the Oregon Senate elect their President. Additional officers include the President Pro-Tem, Majority Leader, and Minority Leader. Senate work in 2022 was performed by 12 Committees each featuring 5 Senators (three Democrats, two Republicans), who conducted hearings on legislation and made referrals about bills to the full Senate. Oregon's 2022 Senate President is Democrat Peter Courtney of Salem, the longest-serving presiding officer in state history. The President Pro Tempore is James Manning, Jr. (Eugene), Democratic Leader is Rob Wagner (Lake Oswego), and the Republican Leader is Tim Knopp (Bend).

Each chamber of the Legislative Assembly is decorated differently. The Senate Chamber carpet features alternate squares depicting a Chinook salmon (the Oregon state fish) and wheat, representing the state's ties to agriculture. A mural behind the dais where the President conducts business depicts the arrival of a messenger in Salem in 1859 announcing that Congress had formally approved Oregon's accession to the Union.

Image: Oregon Senate Chambers.

Image: Senate Committee hearing on dyslexia, 2017.

The House of Representatives

Like the United States House of Representatives, the Oregon House is elected from single-member districts of equal population. Under the Constitution, Oregon may have between 34-60 Representatives. Expansion of the number of Representatives requires voters to approve an amendment to the Constitution. The presiding officer of the House is the Speaker, elected from among the members. Additional officers include the Speaker Pro-Tem, Majority Leader, and Minority Leader. House work in 2022 was performed by 17 Committees featuring between 7-11 members with majority Democrats (except conduct, which has equal membership). Oregon's 2022 Speaker is Dan Rayfield of Corvallis. The President Pro Tempore is Paul Holvey of Eugene, the Democratic Leader is Julie Fahey of Eugene, and the Republican leader is Vikki Breese Iverson of Prineville. The House floor carpet is decorated with pictures of the Douglas Fir, Oregon's state tree. A mural behind the Speaker's dais depicts the Champoeg meetings.

Image: House Chambers

Legislative Sessions

The Oregon Legislative Assembly only held regular sessions in odd years until 2013, conducting business from February until July. In 2012, voters passed a Constitutional Amendment requiring the Legislative Assembly to meet for 35 days in even years, usually from February until March. In between each Regular Session, the Legislative Assembly is organized in an Interim Session, with chambers meeting only during scheduled "Legislative Days" to conduct official business as needed. Special Sessions may be called by the Governor or the Legislative Assembly as needed.

Joint Committees

Several policy arenas are so important that they require the cooperation of members of both chambers of the Legislative Assembly. Several Joint Committees guide the work of the legislature, featuring Senators and Representatives appointed by the presiding officer of their respective chamber.

The most powerful committee is the Joint Committee on Ways & Means, which writes the two-year state budget. Every two years, the Committee conducts hearings in different communities around the state to assess budget priorities. After the hearings are completed, the Committee holds additional meetings in Salem before finally passing the budget. Any bill with fiscal implications must also be passed by the Committee. Portions of the budget are drafted by subcommittees, including Capitol Construction, Education, General Government, Human Services, Natural Resources, Public Safety, and Transportation & Economic Development. The 2022 Co-Chairs are Senator Elizabeth Steiner Hayward and Representative Tawna Sanchez.

How A Bill Becomes Law

The process of bringing community concerns to life as legislation is long, and expert help is often required to assure passage. Individuals professionally employed to pass laws are called "lobbyists," and they are primarily regulated by the Government Ethics Commission and their own self-policing association, the Oregon Capitol Club. Passing a bill can take as long as two years depending on the circumstances.

In 2019, the author advocated for the passage of three bills by the Legislative Assembly. The author's efforts during this process serve the reader as a guide for how legislation is successfully passed as well as killed. For the full narrative, turn to chapter 8.

Image: Rep. John Huffman teaches college students about the legislative process, 2017.

Bill Timeline: SB 394, 2019

February 2018: The author met with legislators in Salem to discuss telecommunications legislation.
Fall 2018: Legislative staff prepared legislative concepts.
January 2019: SB 394 introduced. First reading is followed by President Peter Courtney's referral to the Senate Business and General Government Committee.
February 2019: The Senate Committee holds its public hearing, where the author testified in favor. Later that month, the Committee held its work session when it voted to return the bill to the Senate with a do-pass recommendation.
March 2019: The Senate holds is second and third readings of SB 394. Bill passes unanimously. Following its first reading in the House of Representatives, Speaker Tina Kotek refers the bill to the House Veterans and Emergency Preparedness Committee.
May 2019: The House Committee holds its public hearing and work session on the same day, sending it back to the House with a do-pass recommendation. The Bill passes the House unanimously, and is signed by the Speaker and President.
June 2016: Governor Kate Brown signs SB 394 into law.
January 2020: SB 394 goes into effect.

Chapter 3: The Capitol

While the first government meetings in Oregon were held in the fields of Champoeg, most legislative hearings have occurred inside several different structures. In most states, the building where the legislature meets is called the capitol.

In 2022, the Oregon State Capitol is in the City of Salem. The capital city of Oregon shifted between Salem, Oregon City, and Corvallis a few times. Euegene won a territory-wide election to become the capital in the 1850's, but the results were ignored. Sodaville was shortlisted for state capital due to its size at the time, but lost to Salem. The Oregon State Constitution designates Marion County as the seat of government, and its county seat of Salem as the state capital since 1855.

Image: Salem skyline as seen from the Peter Courtney Minto Island Bridge.

Salem's First Capitol

The first Capitol building to be located in Salem was constructed between 1854-1855. While the Territorial Legislature passed a bill declaring Salem the capital on December 15, 1855, the Capitol burned down on December 29. From 1855-1876, the Territorial and State legislatures met in the Holman Building in downtown Salem, which was later demolished.

Salem's Second Capitol

The Legislative Assembly authorized construction of a new Capitol in 1872, and the building was constructed between 1873-1876. From 1876-1935, the Capitol housed the legislature and other important government offices. Its most famous visitor was President Teddy Roosevelt, who toured the Capitol in 1903.

The Capitol burned down in April 1935, resulting in damage to the nearby Oregon Supreme Court building connected via underground tunnels. A still anonymous witness found the burnt US flag that had flown above the Capitol and delivered it to first responders. The flag is displayed for public viewing in a hearing room in the current Oregon Capitol.

Image: Second Capitol US Sate Flag.

Image: Second Capitol Columns.

Government Buildings

The Oregon State Capitol overlooks the Capitol Mall, which is flanked on both sides by important government buildings. Facing north on the mall is the Oregon State Library, adjacent to the Bureau of Labor & Industries. Two general purpose government office buildings face the mall from the south housing various government offices.

1. Bureau of Labor and Industries
2. Department of Employment
3. Department of Revenue
4. Department of Transportation
5. Public Services Building

Floor By Floor: Ground Floor

The Capitol has five floors with various offices and functions. Most occupants of the Ground Floor would describe it more like a basement, though there are two outdoor meeting spaces with tables, chairs, and plants.

Offices located on the Ground Floor include Information Services, Facility Services, and Legislative Media. Oregon's lobbyist association, the Capitol Club, is located here. Occupants and visitors alike head to this floor for meals at the Cafe, or to testify in Hearing Room 50, the largest hearing room in the building.

Image: Ground floor rest area facing the House Wing.

Floor By Floor: Floor One

Walking up the front Capitol steps lands all visitors in the Rotunda. This special entrance into the Capitol is decorated with murals of famous scenes from Oregon history. Walking to the left, visitors will see offices for the Oregon State Police's Capitol Mall Patrol and Secretary of State. Turning right, visitors will see the State Treasurer and Commission on Indian Services offices.

Moving forward past the gift shop, which is full of Oregon-made gifts, visitors will enter the Galleria, a sparsely-decorated area that usually features rotating historical displays and booths for interest groups. The back hallway behind the gallery is flanked by six hearing rooms. Visitors who walk to the left will see the Legislative Counsel's office, while going right will lead to the Legislative Fiscal office and two additional hearing rooms.

Image: T-shirt on sale in the Capitol Gift Shop.

Floor By Floor: Floor Two

The second floor houses both meeting chambers for the House and Senate. Going left from the Rotunda outside the Capitol steps, visitors ascend a grand staircase leading to the Senate. A duplicate grand staircase leading to the House Chambers faces opposite the Senate stairs. In between the Chambers lies the Governor's ceremonial office, and the business offices where their staff works. The hallway outside the Meeting Chambers and Governor's office is decorated with paintings of several Oregon Governors.

The Speaker of the House's office is behind the House Chamber along with other legislative staff. Several legislative offices are located behind the Senate Chamber, while the President's office is located in the adjacent Senate Wing. Both Chambers have lobby areas where legislators leave floor sessions to meet with lobbyists and constituents. Lobbyists are barred from entering the hallways alongside the floor where each chamber meets during floor sessions.

Floor By Floor: Floor Three

Floor Three is the best place to watch legislators in action. Both Chambers are flanked by decks on the side and galleries above the back of the chamber with ample seating. Several legislators have their offices in the adjacent House and Senate Wings. While the Majority Caucuses have offices on Floor Two, Minority Caucuses have offices on Floor Three. The offices of Legislative Policy & Research are also located on this floor.

Image: View of a chamber choir performance on the Senate floor from the Gallery.

Floor By Floor: Floor Four

Floor Four is usually the least busy of the floors, mainly housing legislators and their staff. Additional office space is used by Legislative Policy and Research, while the Legislative Library and Committee Records room are also located here.

Legislative offices are small. On the House side, each Representative receives space for two desks and a small room for the Representative. Senate offices are double in size to house additional staff and a larger room for the Senator.

Image: Legislative office exterior, Oregon State Capitol.

Chapter 4: Courts & Public Safety

The first individual to serve as a judge in Oregon was Ira Babcock, who held the title of Supreme Judge in a position that also acted as the region's chief executive. A judiciary was created by the Provisional Government that was never organized to the point of functionality.

Congress finally created a Supreme Court for the Territory in 1848. This court consisted of three judges who also traveled throughout the territory to perform judicial functions as trial judges.

The Oregon State Supreme Court was established by the Constitution in 1859 once Congress admitted Oregon into the Union. Oregon's Supreme Court consists of 7 justices elected in statewide nonpartisan elections for six-years terms. One justice is elected to serve as the Chief Justice for a six-year term.

107 judges have served on the Oregon Supreme Court since 1848. Justices commonly retire prior to the end of their term, and their replacements are appointed by the Governor. Usually, justices do not venture into politics outside of judicial races. As noted in Chapter 1, Ted Kuolongoski served as a Supreme Court Justice and State Legislator, as well as Attorney General and Governor.

2022 Oregon Supreme Court

- Chief Justice Martha Lee Walters (Chief Justice since 2018; Associate Justice since 2006)
- Associate Justice Thomas Balmer (since 2001)
- Associate Justice Megan Flynn (since 2017)
- Associate Justice Rebecca Duncan (since 2017)
- Associate Justice Adrienne Nelson (since 2018)
- Associate Justice Christopher Garrett (since 2019)
- Associate Justice Roger DeHoog (since 2022)

Image: Oregon Supreme Court under construction in 2022.

Oregon Court of Appeals

The Oregon Court of Appeals is a statewide elected judiciary that reviews appeals of all decisions made by lower courts on matters other than taxes. This body is composed of 13 justices elected in statewide nonpartisan elections for six-year terms. Oregon's Chief Justice appoints the Chief Judge of the Court of Appeals.

2022 Oregon Court of Appeals

Chief Judge Erin Lagesen (Chief Judge since 2022, Judge since 2013)
Judge Darlene Ortega (since 2003)
Judge James Egan (since 2003)
Judge Douglas Tookey (since 2013)
Judge Scott Shorr (since 2016)
Judge Bronson James (since 2017)
Judge Robyn Aoyagi (since 2017)
Judge Steven Powers (since 2017)
Judge Josephine Mooney (since 2019)
Judge Jacqueline Kamins (since 2020)
Judge Ramón A. Pagán (since 2022)
Judge Kristina Hellman (since 2022)
Judge Anna Joyce (since 2022)

Oregon Tax Court

The Oregon Tax Court is led by one elected Tax Court Judge chosen in statewide nonpartisan elections for a six-year term. Oregon's Tax Court Judge Robert Manicke was elected in 2018. Tax litigation is first heard in the Magistrate Division by magistrates appointed by the Tax Court Judge, then appealed to the Regular Division for an opinion from the Tax Court Judge. Tax Court decisions may be appealed to the Oregon Supreme Court.

Judicial Circuit Courts

Most criminal and civil trials in Oregon are handled by the 27 Circuit Courts. These bodies have at least one judge elected by the communities they serve. While circuit courts often meet in County Courthouses, Circuit Courts are state entities rather than instruments of local government.

Image: Tenth Judicial Circuit Courthouse, La Grande.

Oregon State Police

Oregon's statewide police force is the Oregon State Police. This agency is primarily concerned with providing assistance to local county sheriff offices and city police departments. Areas of enforcement usually involve transportation safety, major crimes, and Special Weapons and Tactics (SWAT) team operations. OSP is also the local point of contact with the Department of Homeland Security. Agency subdivisions include:

Criminal Justice Information Systems and Law Enforcement Data Systems
Fish and Wildlife Division
Forensic Services Division
Gaming Division
Office of the Chief Medical Examiner
Patrol Services Division
Office of State Fire Marshal

Retired Oregon State Police officers serve as plain-clothes security in the Oregon State Capitol during the legislative session. Plain-clothes agents in the Dignitary Protection Unit are assigned to protect the Governor and the Governor-elect after an election is held.

Image: Oregon Fallen Law Enforcement Memorial.

County Courts

Several other entities in Oregon have the title of Court. A few County Board of Commissioners with smaller populations are organized as a County Court, with a Judge elected by their constituents who serves as the presiding officer at meetings of Commissioners. This type of County Judge also handles probate issues, adoptions, guardianship, conservatorships, and juvenile issues.

Justice Courts may be created by County Commissioners with jurisdiction over traffic, boating, and wildlife in the county. Municipal Courts are established by City Councils, primarily to hear matters regarding traffic; municipal codes and ordinance violations; vehicle impoundments; and parking and pedestrian violations. They may also hear specified liquor and drug violations. County residents elect a Justice of the Peace; no municipal judge in Oregon is elected. Elgin has an appointed municipal judge. In Linn County, most cities contract with the Justice of the Peace to serve as Municipal Judge.

Image: Sherman County Courthouse in Moro, seat of County Court.

County Sheriffs

Every county in Oregon elects a Sheriff who serves as the chief law enforcement officer in unincorporated areas. Sheriffs provide bailiff services to the Circuit Courts. Local jails are operated by most Sheriff Departments. County Sheriffs also commonly contract with small cities and other local governments to provide local law enforcement. In Union County, the cities of Elgin and Union contract with the Sheriff's Department for local law enforcement services. The La Grande School District contracts with the Union County Sheriff to provide a School Resource Officer assigned to protecting students and building relationships that encourage youth to avoid criminal behavior.

City Police Departments

Many cities in Oregon employ their own police forces. Police Departments are led by a Chief of Police who often acts as a higher-level manager in city government. The Oregon Association of Chiefs of Police provides local law enforcement leaders with special training and advocates in Salem and Washington, DC.

Fire Safety

Local fire protection is primarily provided by either of two entities: city police departments, or rural fire protection districts (RFPD). City fire departments are funded and managed by city governments, often in communities with larger populations and thus higher property tax revenue. RFPD's are special districts that collect their own property taxes or service charges, governed by a locally elected board of directors.

The Oregon Department of Forestry operates Oregon's largest fire department, responsible for protecting 16 million acres of forest valued at $60 billion. ODF firefighters also fight fires on land owned by the Bureau of Land Management on the western side of the state. The US Forest Service is in charge of fighting fire on lands owned by this agency.

Image: Elgin RFPD hosts pancake breakfast fundraiser, 2020.

Military

Oregonians are protected by several key state military forces. The Oregon Military Department is led by an Adjutant General appointed by the Governor, who is officially the commander in chief of state military forces. Oregon's three military components are the Army National Guard, Air National Guard, and Civil Defense Force.

Oregon Army National Guard

The Oregon Army National Guard is Oregon's local reserve infantry component of the United States Army. During peacetime, the National Guard is under the command of the Governor, the commander in chief chosen by voters. Commonly, the National Guard assists in natural disaster recovery. Under federal law, State National Guards may be placed under the command of the President of the United States at any time and deployed to assist in domestic issues or sent overseas for combat and peacekeeping missions.

Oregon Air National Guard

Much like the Army National Guard, the Air National Guard is Oregon's local air reserved component of the United States Air Force. During peacetime, the Air National Guard is under the command of the Governor. The Oregon Air National Guard was created in 1941.

Oregon Civil Defense Force

States are allowed to operate reserve forces outside of the control of the US Armed Forces. Oregon organized its own state militia during the American Civil War to protect frontier communities in the absence of the US Army. The Oregon National Guard Reserve was formed in 1961 and renamed the Oregon State Defense Force in 1989. The SDF was suspended in 2015 and relaunched in 2019 as the Oregon Civil Defense Force. ORCDF members do not wear military fatigues, instead donning plain clothes with a patch identifying their allegiance. The CDF's main mission is maintaining National Guard telecommunications equipment.

Chapter 5: Local Government

Oregon has three primary levels of local government: counties, cities, and special districts. All of these entities are governed and organized by state statute and governed by local elected official. In 1843, the first four Oregon counties were organized in Clackamas, Marion, Washington, and Yamhill Counties. Oregon City was officially incorporated in 1844. Special districts have operated in Oregon for decades, with the Special Districts Association founded in 1979. The rarest type of local government are intergovernmental agencies organized under ORS Chapter 190.

Counties

Oregon's 36 counties provide municipal services to communities that are not served by cities. They also perform duties prescribed by state law and receive grants from the federal government to perform specific services. The largest Oregon County by population is Multnomah with 815,428 residents, and the largest by area is Harney at 10,135 square miles. Oregon's smallest county by population is Wheeler with 1,451 residents, while Multnomah is the smallest by territory at 435 square miles.

County Government

Most counties are governed by elected Boards of Commissioners. Some Counties directly elect a commission chair, while other counties rotate the chairmanship between members annually. Small counties are governed by County Courts consisting of a Judge, who acts as the presiding officer, and two Commissioners. Boards of Commissioners have either three or five members.

All counties include several specialized elected offices, some of which may be combined. County Clerks oversee elections, maintain county records, and issue marriage licenses. Tax Collectors collect revenue, Assessors value property, and Surveyors survey land. Treasurers manage and distribute County funds. Some offices are combined: in Union County, the Assessor and Tax Collector are one office, while Baker County combines the Treasurer and Tax Collector.

Oregon Counties possess a great deal of autonomy when enacting policies that address local concerns. County residents may enter into either Constitutional or Statutory Home Rule, which has two objectives: the ability to enact local legislation without authorization by state law, and the ability to reorganize county governments. Constitutional home rule is governed by a process established in the Constitution, while the legislature established Statutory Home Rule as an alternative for Counties that sought autonomy despite potential difficulties in achieving Constitutional Home Rule. Of 25 Counties that ever held home rule elections, only nine were successful, and five were ultimately repealed by voters.

County Commissioners are charged with filling vacancies on city councils and special district boards if a majority of seats on these bodies become vacant.

County Boards and Commissions

County Commissioners appoint several board and committee members that advise them on special policy matters. Union County appoints members of 23 committees.

- 4-H and Extension District Advisory Committee
- 4-H and Extension District Budget Committee
- Airport Advisory Committee
- Ambulance District Advisory Committee
- Board of Property Tax Appeals
- Union County Budget Committee
- Buffalo Peak Golf Course Advisory Committee
- Union County Community Forest Restoration Board
- Union County Fair Association Board of Directors
- Health & Human Services Advisory Committee
- Hospital Facility Authority of Union County
- Household Hazardous Waste Steering Committee
- Mt. Emily Recreation Area Motorized Advisory Committee
- Mt. Emily Recreation Area Non-Motorized Advisory Committee
- Northeast Area Commission on Transportation
- Union County Planning Commission
- Special Transportation Fund (STF) Advisory Committee
- Transient Tax Advisory Committee
- Union County Transportation Committee
- Vector Control District Board of Directors
- Vector Control District Budget Committee
- Weed Control Advisory Committee
- Wolf Depredation Compensation Committee

District Attorneys

Oregon's District Attorneys are lawyers who prosecute crimes committed in their respective counties. District Attorneys are assisted by several deputies. All District Attorneys function as state officials though elected locally. A District Attorney partially functions as a county official, with salaries funded by both the state and the County they represent. County courthouses often maintain headquarters for County District Attorneys.

County Associations

Oregon's counties unite to serve their citizens in a forum called the Association of Oregon Counties. This organization provides training to city officials, operates an insurance pool for municipal employees, and lobbies in Salem. AOC is a member of the National Association of Counties. In 2022, the AOC Co-Chairs are Multnomah County Commissioner Susheela Jayapal and Tillamook County Commissioner David Yamamoto. The Eastern Oregon Counties Association is composed of rural counties that primarily advocate together on forest policy.

Image: Joseph Building, Union County government offices, La Grande.

Cities

Oregon has 241 cities, with 14 of these cities incorporated in the territory of multiple counties. Cities are often the most visible manifestations of local government, providing street maintenance, water delivery, park operations, and other services. The largest city in Oregon by population (652,503) and land area (145 square miles) is Portland. The smallest city by area is Barlow in Clackamas County (.5 square miles), while the smallest by population is Greenhorn in Baker and Grant Counties. Incorporated Greenhorn has no permanent population, with homeowners registering to vote there to serve on the City Council but residing elsewhere in Oregon.

City Councils

Cities are governed by an elected City Council or City Commission, and all cities have a Mayor. Councils usually have either five or seven members. Pendleton has eight City Councilors, two each elected from equal-population districts called "wards," and two elected at-large from the entire city. Hillsboro's six Councilors are elected from within three wards, but are elected by all voters regardless of their respective ward.

Image: Sodaville City Hall.

Mayors

The Mayor is usually the presiding officer of the City Council, with no administrative duties. Portland's Mayor is the presiding officer of the City Board of Commissioners, chief executive of the city government, and commissioner overseeing multiple city agencies. Under La Grande's Charter, the Mayor's only express role besides presiding over Council meetings is appointing members of the city's various commissions, all of which must be approved by the Council. In Baker City, the Mayor is chosen from among one of the City Councilors serving as presiding officer for two years out of the four-year Council term. Only Beaverton and Portland elect Mayors as full-time chief executives. In 2022, the President of the Oregon Mayors Association is Cottage Grove Mayor Jeff Gowing.

City Managers

Almost all Oregon City Councils appoint a city manager, who serves as the chief administrative official on behalf of the Council. Elgin is the only city with an elected city manager. Some cities entitle their chief administrative officer "City Recorder," a title that is almost always semantic in that context and may have been used historically. Several cities appoint both a City Manager and a City Recorder. In these cases, the City Manager serves as the chief administrator, while the Recorder is the secretary to the City Council, record keeper, and elections officer. In 2022, the President of the Oregon City/County Managers Association is Gervais City Manager Susie Marston. The 2020-2022 President of the Oregon Association of Municipal Recorders is Harrisburg Deputy City Recorder Cathy Nelson.

City Boards and Commissions

All Oregon cities must appoint at least one volunteer body that performs official work advising the Council or the work of city staff. Every city must appoint a budget committee consisting of all Council members and a number of volunteers equivalent to the number of Councilors. If a Council includes the Mayor and four Councilors, the Budget Committee must include the Mayor, four Councilors, and five volunteers. City Planning Commissions make decisions about construction and zoning that are considered final unless appealed to the City Council. The City of Lebanon's standing committees include the Budget; Library Advisory; Parks, Trees, and Trails Advisory; Senior & Disabled Services Advisory; and Planning Commission.

League of Oregon Cities

Oregon's cities unite to serve their citizens in a forum called the League of Oregon Cities. This organization provides training to city officials, operates an insurance pool for municipal employees, and lobbies in Salem. LOC jointly operates an insurance pool, City/County Insurance Services, with the Association of Oregon Counties. The 2022 President of LOC is Central Point City Councilor Taneea Browning. The Chair of CIS is Dallas City Councilor Kenneth Woods, serving with Vice Chair Tyler Stone, Wasco County Administrative Officer.

Special Districts

The other type of non-education local government in Oregon is a special district. These local governments are created by voters to provide specific services in areas where a city government may not exist or may be unable to provide necessary services. The community of Elgin is served by a City, along with Fire Protection, Parks, Health, and Cemetery Maintenance districts that cannot be operated by the City.

SDAO

Similar to the Association of Oregon Counties and League of Oregon Cities, Oregon's special districts are represented by the Special Districts Association of Oregon. This entity provides training for special district officials, operates internal associations for certain types of special districts, advocates for members in Salem, and jointly operates an insurance pool with the Oregon School Boards Association. Oregon is one of only seven states with a statewide association for all special districts, and these seven collectively form the National Special District Coalition. The NSDC advocates on behalf of special districts in Washington, DC. This coalition offers associate membership to statewide associations of specific special districts, such as the Washington Public Ports Association. In 2022, the President of SDAO is Todd Heidgerken, General Manager of Clackamas River Water.

Unfunded Mandates

Under Article XI Section 15 of the Oregon Constitution, the Legislative Assembly may not impose unfunded mandates on cities. This means that if less than ⅗ of legislators vote to task a city or county with an objective, the legislature must also provide funding, or the act cannot be enforced. If a city wishes to appeal a mandate as unfunded, the Constitution requires the matter be submitted to a panel including representatives of the League of Oregon Cities, the Association of Oregon Counties, and the Department of Administrative Services.

Regional Councils

Local governments of all types frequently band together to assist in advocacy on special projects, share information, and offer other services to members. Each Council has its own system of governance. The Oregon Cascade West Council of Governments is overseen by a Board consisting of one elected official from each member government, with each member casting one vote. Oregon has six Regional Councils.

- Central Oregon Intergovernmental Council
- Lane Council of Governments
- Mid-Willamette Valley Council of Governments
- Northwest Senior and Disability Services
- Oregon Cascades West Council of Governments
- Rogue Valley Council of Governments

Metro

Oregon is home to the only regional planning body in America governed by an elected board. The Metro Council consists of a directly elected President elected from across the region, and six Councilors elected from wards with equal population. Metro's Auditor is also directly elected. The agency's list of responsibilities is expansive:

- Patrol regional illegal dumping.
- Provide land-use planning within Portland's Urban Growth Boundary
- Serve as metropolitan planning organization
- Oversee an affordable housing bond
- Plan the region's transportation system
- Maintain the region's Geographic Information System and Regional Land Information System
- Manage 17,000 acres of Portland-area natural areas including ten parks, a boat ramps, a golf course, and a wetland
- Maintain 14 pioneer cemeteries
- Manage a closed landfill
- Operate both regional public garbage, hazardous waste, and recycling transfer stations
- Dispose of the region's solid waste and regulate private transfer stations
- Operate the Oregon Convention Center, Oregon Zoo, Portland Centers for the Arts, and Portland Expo Center
- Metro retains the right to take over operation of the regional transportation authority, TriMet.

Chapter 6: Education

Education is at the foundation of Oregon's prosperity, tied closely to natural resources. In Oregon, all children attend school from Kindergarten to 12th Grade. K-12 graduates may further their education at a trade school, community college, or university.

K-12 Schools

Upon statehood, the federal government granted land to the State for the purpose of harvesting natural resources, using the profits to fund K-12 education. These state lands are governed by the State Land Board, a body composed of the Governor as presiding officer along with the Secretary of State and State Treasurer. The Legislative Assembly is empowered by the Constitution to establish a system of common schools funded by the proceeds of the Common School Fund, with revenue distributed in counties based on their respective populations of schoolchildren. School districts operate campuses from all levels from kindergarten to 12th grade. Schools are also funded by property taxes and gross receipts taxes among other revenue sources.

School Boards

All school districts are governed by elected school boards, whose members are chosen during school board and special district elections during odd years. The powers and duties of school boards are mandated by the Legislative Assembly. School boards are elected to ensure that these institutions are beholden to the needs of local parents whose children are educated. School boards also oversee the appointment and direction of the Superintendent, who serves as the district's chief administrative officer, just like city councils appoint city managers.

The Oregon School Boards Association

Oregon's school boards unite to serve their citizens in a forum called the Oregon School Boards Association. This organization provides training to school officials, operates an insurance pool for school employees, and lobbies in Salem. The 2022 President of OSBA is Scott Rogers, Chair of the Athena-Weston 29J School Board.

Image: North Powder School Board meeting, 2021.

Education Service Districts

School districts that lack the resources to pay for all necessary education services are supported by regional Education Service Districts. The districts are governed by an elected board of directors. All 19 ESD's are members of the Oregon Association of Education Service Districts.

ESD's serve an important continuity of government function normally served to Counties. When a majority of seats on a school board become vacant, the ESD Board is in charge of appointing replacements.

Oregon Department of Education

At a State level, education policy is directed by the Governor as ex officio Superintendent of Public Instruction in charge of the Oregon Department of Education. The position of Superintendent was a statewide elected office from 1874 until its merger with the Governor's office in 2012. The second longest serving statewide elected official in Oregon history was Superintendent Rex Putnam, a Democrat, whose tenure was just 7 months shy of BOLI Commissioner Charles Gram. The Department of Education's daily operations are overseen by the Deputy Superintendent of Public Instruction and governed by the State Board of Education.

Charter Schools

The Oregon Department of Education defines a charter school as "a public school operated by a group of parents, teachers and/or community members as a semi-autonomous school of choice within a school district. It is given the authority to operate under a contract or "charter" between the members of the charter school community and the local board of education (sponsor). Under Oregon law, a charter school is a separate legal entity operating under a binding agreement with a sponsor. A public charter school is subject to certain laws pertaining to school district public schools, is released from others and must operate consistent with the charter agreement." Some school districts include charter schools, such as the Lebanon School District's People Involved in Education campuses. Some school districts only operate charter schools, such as North Powder School District.

Private Schools

The Oregon Department of Education's websites says, "Non-public education is recognized as a vital part of Oregon's educational system. Parents have the option of providing their child's education through Private or Home School. Private schools do not have to register with the State of Oregon, unless they are contracting with public school district for services. Although private pre-12 schools no longer register, the process for Child Care Licensing remains in effect."

Higher Education Coordinating Commission

Oregon is home to the oldest college in the Western United States, Willamette University, established by Oregon founding father Reverend Jason Lee. In Oregon, colleges are generally autonomous institutions, regulated rather than managed by the Higher Education Coordinating Commission. This Commission is appointed by the Governor and the agency is managed by its Executive Director, former State Representative Ben Cannon.

Community Colleges

Oregon's 17 community colleges trace their history back to Central Oregon Community College in Bend, founded in 1949. Under the auspices of the HECC, community colleges are regulated by the Oregon Office of Community Colleges and Workforce Development. Each community college is led by an elected Board of Education. The Oregon Community College Association supports and advocates for the mission of the Beaver States public associate institutions. In 2022, the OCCA President is Kim Morgan, Columbia Gorge Community College trustee. Students organize through the Oregon Community College Students Association.

2022 Oregon Community Colleges

- Blue Mountain Community College (Pendleton)
- Central Oregon Community College (Bend)
- Chemeketa Community College (Salem)
- Clackamas Community College (Oregon City)
- Clatsop Community College (Astoria)
- Columbia Gorge Community College (The Dalles)
- Klamath Community College (Klamath Falls)
- Lane Community College (Eugene)
- Linn-Benton Community College (Albany)
- Mt. Hood Community College (Gresham)
- Oregon Coast Community College (Newport)
- Portland Community College (Portland)
- Rogue Community College (Grants Pass)
- Southwestern Oregon Community College (Coos Bay)
- Tillamook Bay Community College (Tillamook
- Treasure Valley Community College (Ontario)
- Umpqua Community College (Roseburg)

Image: Ways & Means Committee hearing at Blue Mountain Community College, 2019.

Public Universities

Higher education opportunities have been available to Oregonians since the 1840's, and the Legislative Assembly began regulating Oregon universities in 1909. In 1929, the State established the first public higher education institution, Eastern Oregon Normal School, which was later renamed Eastern Oregon State College then Eastern Oregon University. EOU graduates include the author, US Congressman Cliff Bentz, and Micronesian President David Panuelo. EOU and Southern Oregon University share duplicate administration buildings designed by the same architect.

Public universities were managed by the Oregon State Board of Higher Education until 2015, holding its final meeting at Eastern Oregon University. The three "big" universities, Oregon State, Portland State, and University of Oregon, gained autonomy under their own boards in 2014, followed by the Technical and Regional Universities (TRU's) in 2015. Boards are appointed by the Governor and include a student, faculty member, and classified employee. All seven public universities are members of the Oregon Council of Presidents, staffed by Western Oregon University. Student governments organize through the Oregon Student Association, and faculty organize through the Interinstitutional Faculty Senate.

2022 Oregon Public Universities

- Eastern Oregon University (La Grande)
- Oregon Institute of Technology (Klamath Falls)
- OIT Portland-Metro
- Oregon State University (Corvallis)
- OSU-Cascades
- Portland State University (Portland)
- Southern Oregon University (Ashland)
- University of Oregon (Eugene)
- Western Oregon University (Monmouth)

Image: Final meeting, Oregon State Board of Higher Education, 2015.

Image: Eastern Oregon University.

Oregon Health and Science University

Oregon medicinal studies trace their roots back to 1867 when Willamette University founded its School of Medicine. Willamette's program merged with University of Oregon Medical School, and the combined initiative was headquartered in Portland in 1919. Over time, this institute evolved into Oregon Health and Science University, so named in 1981. The President of OHSU participates in the Oregon Council of Presidents alongside the seven public universities.

Private Universities

22 private higher education institutions operate in Oregon in 2022. These colleges are self-governing, but are regulated by the Oregon HECC. Willamette University is the oldest university still operating in Oregon, public or private.

Chapter 7: Oregon Culture

Political Parties

Oregon has three major political parties, defined in statute as maintaining membership of at least 5% of all voters 275 days before a primary. The three Parties meeting this definition are the Democratic Party of Oregon, Independent Party of Oregon, and Oregon Republican Party. The largest voting bloc, however, is non-affiliated voters.

Democratic Party of Oregon

According to their website, "The Democratic Party of Oregon promotes the election of Democratic candidates at every level across the state of Oregon with technical and volunteer support. We provide opportunities for all Oregon Democrats to participate fully in our political process. The Democratic Party of Oregon supports local county Parties to make sure that every community can work to get Democratic Candidates elected." The Democratic Caucus in the 81st Legislative Assembly includes 18 Senators and 37 Representatives.

2022 Officers

- Chair KC Hanson
- Vice Chair Pete Lee
- Vice Chair Rosa Colquitt
- Secretary Eileen Kiely
- Treasurer Eddy Morales
- National Committee Member Michelle Risher
- National Committee Member Travis Nelson

- National Committee Member Matt Keating

Oregon Republican Party

According to their platform, "the Republican Party of Oregon stand[s] for our Country as one nation under God, our Creator, for life, liberty, and the pursuit of happiness. We believe each generation should teach, proclaim, promote and defend the essential civic Virtues of our founding. As free people, all Oregonians have the opportunity, through hard work and perseverance, to build a more prosperous future for themselves, their families, and their communities, without the excessive burden of government." The Republican Caucus in the 81st Legislative Assembly includes 11 Senators and 23 Representatives.

2022 Officers

- Chair Justin Hwang
- Vice Chair Angela Plowhead
- Secretary Becky Mitts
- Treasurer Alex McHaddad
- National Committeeman Solomon Yue
- National Committeewoman Tracy Honl

Image: Senator Dallas Heard Chairs the ORP Central Committee, 2021.

Independent Party of Oregon

According to their platform, the Independent Party asks, "our members what issues they would like us to prioritize and we construct a platform that meets the public interest goals they have articulated. We do this by reviewing current policies as well as policies under consideration in light of public opinion research, academic research and policies that have been enacted in other jurisdictions. We also take feedback from policy experts and thought leaders during the drafting process." The 81st Legislative Assembly includes one Independent Party Senator. The Party often cross-nominates candidates with the other major parties, though only one partisan elected official has ever retained the party identity while in office.

2022 Officers

Co-Chair Drew Karza
Co-Chair Dan Meek
Co-Chair Linda Williams
Co-Chair Ken Smith
Secretary Sal Peralta
Treasurer Joan Horton

Minor Parties

Oregon's other political parties include the Progressive Party and Working Families Party. National parties with minor party affiliates include the Constitution Party, Libertarian Party, and Pacific Green Party (affiliate of the Green Party).

Organized Labor

As the first state to officially celebrate Labor Day, Oregon's history is closely tied to the work of its laborers. The first labor organization formed in the Northwest was the Oregon and Washington Typographical Society, established in 1853. Oregon's first recorded strike occurred in 1869 at the Dalles mint, while the Harness Makers Association organized the first successful strike in state history in 1880.

Industry

Oregon is home to five 2022 Fortune 500 companies: Columbia Sportswear, Lithia Motors, Nike, Portland General Electric, and Schnitzer Steel Industries.

The Portland area hosts an array of big tech companies, earning the name "Silicon Forest." Tech firms operating in the Silicon Forest include Epson, HP, InFocus, Intel, Planar Systems, Pixelworks, Tektronix, and Xerox.

Plentiful renewable energy draws increasing tech investment over time. Google's first owned and operated data center is in The Dalles, where company owner Alphabet has invested over $1.8 billion since 2006. Google.org has donated over $14 million in grants in Oregon since 2009, and since 2006, Google's Oregon employees have donated over $3 million to charity with employer matching. In Prineville, Facebook and Apple have each invested over $1 billion in data centers and the local economy.

Newspapers

110 print newspapers are in general circulation in Oregon, with most counties served by at least one local paper. Oregon's largest newspaper, *The Oregonian*, has been in circulation since 1850.

TV Stations

Television first came to Oregon in 1952, with broadcaster KPTV as the first commercial station in the nation to broadcast in the Ultra High Frequency (UHF) band. Oregon has 35 full-power TV stations, 50 low-power TV stations, and 197 translators.

Oregon Public Broadcasting serves as Oregon's Public Broadcasting Station and National Public Radio affiliate. OPB broadcasts international, national, and local news, also producing local content aired around America.

Oregon Counties are divided into designated market areas that determine which local TV stations broadcast in their territory:
- Bend: Deschutes
- Boise: Grant and Malheur Counties
- Eugene: Benton, Coos, Douglas, and Lane Counties
- Medford: Curry, Harney, Jackson, Josephine, and Lake Counties
- Portland: All other Counties
- Spokane: Wallowa County
- Yakima: Morrow and Umatilla Counties

Image: Signpost for KTVR, an OPB transmitter, in Union County.

National Parkland

Oregon's only National Park is Crater Lake, located in Klamath County. The park was established in 1902, encompassing a mountaintop lake that formed in the caldera of a volcanic eruption. Oregon has 106 federal protected areas, including Parks, Historic Parks and Sites, Monuments and Forests, Grasslands and Recreation Areas, Wildlife Refuges, Wildernesses, Conservation Lands, Wild & Scenic Rivers, and other protected areas.

State Parks

The Oregon Parks and Recreation Department operates 193 facilities, including beaches, boat launches, campgrounds, guided ocean viewpoints, heritage areas, interpretive centers, national historic landmarks, natural areas, recreation areas and sites, rest areas, scenic corridors and viewpoints, parks, trails, and waysides. The very first Oregon State Park was in Sodaville, Oregon, now owned by the City of Sodaville. This Park consisted of a bathhouse above a soda spring, which was used for both bathing and drinking due to hypothesized medicinal properties.

Image: Smith Rock State Park.

Oregon Films

Films have been produced in Oregon since 1897's *Fast Mail, Northern Pacific Railroad*, shot in Portland. 455 films are known to have been shot in Oregon, most recently Guillermo del Toro's *Pinocchio* (2022). The arguably most famous film shot in Oregon is *The Goonies*, filmed on location in Astoria, Oregon. The film's "jailbreak" scene was filmed at the old Clatsop County Jail, which now houses the Oregon Film Museum. *One Flew Over the Cuckoo's Nest* was filmed at the Oregon State Hospital. Stop-motion animation producer Laika Studios in Hillsboro, established by Nike co-founder Phil Knight, produced *Coraline* and *ParaNorman*, among others.

Oregon Literature

There is no conclusive list of Oregonian authors or books published in Oregon. Several famous authors have called Oregon home. Beverly Cleary, famous for children's novels featuring the protagonist Ramona Quimby, was born in McMinville and spent her life in Portland. California-born fantasy author Ursula K. Le Guin, best-known for the *Earthsea* series, moved to Portland in 1859. *One Flew Over the Cuckoo's Nest* was written by Lane County-based author Ken Kesey.

Image: Oregon State Library lobby.

Oregon Beer

Every Oregonian knows that the heart of many Beaver State towns is its brewpub. Even for those who do not partake in the hundreds of craft beers produced in Oregon, brewpubs often serve as gathering places and the pinnacle of dining options in small towns. Breweries have operated in Oregon since 1854, and 48 breweries are currently in operation all across the state.

Oregon Wine

Oregon vineyards have produced wine since 1840, and the industry gained significance starting in the 1960's. The Oregon Wine Board was established by the legislature in 2003, consisting of nine members appointed by the Governor. The Board's responsibility is to recommend labeling standards for Oregon wines to the Oregon Liquor and Cannabis Commission, as well as support the development and promotion of Oregon wines. Oregon is divided into seven American Viticultural Areas, Willamette Valley, Southern Oregon, Umpqua Valley, Rogue Valley, Columbia Gorge, Columbia Valley, and Snake River.

Oregon Cannabis

Oregon voters legalized the production, possession, and sale of recreational marijuana in 2014. Marijuana and liquor are both regulated by the Oregon Liquor and Cannabis Commission.

Image: Oregon cannabis competition at the 2016 Oregon State Fair.

Hunting

Harvesting natural resources directly for food has been a necessity for Oregonians since the arrival of indigenous peoples. The Oregon Department of Fish and Wildlife regulates hunting and conservation efforts, offering tags for black bears, cougars, deer, elk, bighorn sheep, pronghorn antelope, and Rocky Mountain goats. ODFW also offers game bird tags for waterfowl, band-tailed pigeons, sage grouse, sea ducks, turkeys, and pheasants. Oregon hunters have organized as the Oregon Hunters Association since 1983, promoting hunting ,conservation, and education. OHA also offers financial rewards for tips leading to the arrest of poachers.

Fishing

Oregon salmon and other fish have fed Beaver State residents since the arrival of indigenous people. ODFW regulates fishing licenses, offering tags for salmon, steelhead, sturgeon, and halibut. Crabbing and clamming are just as popular, with ODFW offering tags for collecting these sea creatures.

Foraging

A complete sampling of an Oregonian dinner table is incomplete without at least some vegetables next to a slice of turkey, an elk steak, a razor clam, and a local craft IPA. During summer, Oregonians love foraging for fruits and vegetables. Huckleberries make fine snacks and deserts, while morels are eaten on their own, in salads, or ground within sausage.

Chapter 8: How a Bill Becomes Law

The process of bringing community concerns to life as legislation is long, and expert help is often required to assure passage. Individuals professionally employed to pass laws are called "lobbyists," and they are primarily regulated by the Government Ethics Commission and their own self-policing association, the Oregon Capitol Club. Passing a bill can take as long as two years depending on the circumstances. In 2019, the author advocated for the passage of three bills. The author's efforts during this process will serve the reader as a guide for how legislation is successfully passed as well as killed.

Reforming A Special District

From 2017-2021, the author served as the manager of Oregon's last translator district, a unique local government agency that operates TV repeater stations in Baker and Union Counties. Translator district funds primarily came from voluntary service charges, punitive tax liens, and technical partnerships, resulting in unpredictable revenue. Administrative provisions in state law also made the management of the district difficult. Three bills were introduced to ensure that at least one legislative change was signed into law.

- **SB 393: Administration.** Translator district boundaries could not legally include cities, so the district boundaries spanned the length of two counties but the map had large "donut holes" around ten cities. Residents of these cities could be affected by the District, but could not serve on the Board. This bill allowed voters in cities surrounded by a translator district to vote on annexation, and permitted city residents who paid the service charge to serve on the Board of Directors.
- **SB 394: Technology.** This bill allowed translator districts to generate revenue by operating their own TV stations and broadcast using next-generation standards, which brought other revenue-generating opportunities.
- **SB 901: Ad Valorem Property Taxes.** Translator district voters must vote to enact a service charge system that requires all district property owners and the owners of properties in cities with an antenna to pay a fee to watch over-the-air TV. They may request an exemption, but if they don't reply within at least 30 days by statute, the charge is enrolled on their property taxes as a lien the following year. When passing the original translator district revenue statutes, the Legislative Assembly required voters to approve the system but also decreed that the one existing translator district already had voter approval for the system despite an election not occurring. This bill would have allowed voters to finally choose between the service charge system or levying ad valorem property taxes.

Legislative Sponsors

All bills must be sponsored by at least one member of each chamber by the time they go to the floor. In 2018, the author discussed potential translator district legislation with Senator Bill Hansell and Representative Greg Barreto, who represented Union County, along with Senator Cliff Bentz and Representative Lynn Findley, who represented Baker County. During the 2019 session, Senator Bentz was the Chief Sponsor of all three bills. Representatives Barreto and Findely were Regular Sponsors of Senate Bills 393 and 394.

Legislative Concepts

Once a list of policies was identified, they were sent to the Office of Legislative Counsel. This is the legislative agency that officially writes bills to ensure that they comply with the US and Oregon Constitutions along with applicable federal and state law. Legislative Concepts were introduced as SB 393 and SB 394 at the beginning of the 2019 Legislative Session. SB 901 was introduced later.

Community Feedback

The author had to secure community support for SB 393 and SB 394 in order to convince legislative committees to recommend the bills to the floor of their respective Chambers. SB 394 had the most buy-in from the community, receiving letters of support from the Baker and Union County Boards of Commissioners; North Powder, Island City, Elgin, Imbler, Baker City, and Haines City Councils; La Grande and Union Rural Fire Protection Districts; the Union County Farm Bureau; and the Union County Chamber of Commerce. SB 393 was supported by the Baker and Union County Commissioners, along with all cities except Island City. SB 901 was ultimately only supported by the Union County Board of Commissioners.

Both the author and members of the translator district board attended several local government meetings to discuss legislation with public bodies. Some local governments requested to discuss the legislation at multiple meetings. Meetings took place in venues ranging from historic courthouses in the morning to wilderness firehouses late at night.

Image: The author with the firehouse dog at Keating Rural Fire HQ.

Image: The Elgin City Council deliberates supporting SB 393 and SB 394.

Committee Assignment and Hearings

The author met with the offices of a majority of Senators, usually interfacing with staff. After a meeting with the office of Senate President Peter Courtney, it was determined that SB 393 and SB 394 would be referred to the Senate Committee on Business & General Government. Under Senate rules, the President is given authority over whether bills are brought to the floor and referred to a Committee, and the referral process was smooth. After the author met with Chair Rod Monroe, the Business & General Government Committee scheduled a public hearing on both bills. The author sent letters from supportive community partners to the Committee and worked with the Legislative Policy & Revenue Office to provide the Committee with adequate updates.

The Public Hearing on SB 393 and 394 was held on February 7. The author summarized the bills alongside a PowerPoint presentation followed by questions from the five Committee members. Only one Committee member seemed opposed to the passage of the bills. Ultimately, the Committee held a work session on February 21 and unanimously voted to refer SB 394 back to the floor with a "Do pass" recommendation.

Image: Testimony on SB 393 & 394, Oregon State Capitol, 2019.

Each bill that enters a legislative chamber ultimately receives three "readings," either in full or by title only. The first reading occurs when the presiding officer introduces the bill. The second reading occurs after a committee has moved the bill to the floor. The third reading occurs when the chamber votes on passage.

Senator Bentz discussed the details of the bill with the author before "carrying" it on the floor, a process that entailed him summarizing the legislation and potentially taking questions from fellow Senators prior to the vote. SB 394 passed the Senate with the "Aye" votes of all 25 present Senators, and it moved to the House.

Image: Senate votes to pass SB 394, Oregon State Capitol, March 4, 2019.

A helpful tool educating legislators about translator districts was a Courtesy of the Senate extended to the author during a floor session. Senator Bill Hansell recognized the author from the floor with a short speech about the work of managing Oregon's only translator district before asking the Senate to extend its courtesies. Members of both chambers commonly ensure that their visiting constituents receive this special recognition.

Image: An Eastern Oregon University Trustee receives courtesies of the Senate, 2017.

SB 393's progress was impeded by the late introduction of SB 901. Because SB 393 would have allowed voters to potentially annex cities into a translator district, and SB 901 would have allowed voters to levy property taxes, the legislature was obligated to spend more time examining the passage of two bills that would potentially increase property tax burdens for residents of ten cities in two counties.

Amendments were requested to SB 393 to ensure that annexation elections could not be held until after 2020 when adequate community feedback had occurred, and exempted state properties from service charges. Most state-owned properties in Oregon are exempted from property taxes, but those not exempt are also subjected to translator district service charges, and the district had regularly charged state taxpayers hundreds of dollars per year because exemption forms were not signed. SB 393 was amended to prevent state properties from being charged because certain potentially annexed cities would be forced to pay taxes, and the bill was in danger of failing if there was a fiscal impact. SB 901 was amended to require property tax votes to be held during November Presidential elections when voters are most likely to vote, preventing the question from being swept under the rug during a low-profile special district election when turnout is traditionally low.

SB 393 received a "Do pass" recommendation from the Business & General Government Committee with a "Nay" vote from one Senator before its referral to the Finance & Revenue Committee. A public hearing on SB 393 was held on March 19, followed by joint public hearings on SB 393 and 901 on May 21. The Committee ultimately pushed both bills forward on June 5.

Under the Oregon Constitution, bills must be read in full on the floor of their respective chambers unless this is waived by a majority of the chamber. House and Senate Republicans voted against the waiver for much of the session, resulting in several days passing before floor votes on SB 393 and SB 901. SB 393 passed with the unanimous support of all 26 present Senators, while SB 901 received only two "Nay" votes.

Passing legislation in the House was a similar process. SB 394 was referred to the House Committee on Veterans & Emergency Preparedness. Committee Chair Rep. Paul Evans held a public hearing and work session on the same day and offered to carry the bill on the floor, citing an ongoing walkout by Senate Republicans. Rep. Findley, a fellow committee member, reminded Rep. Evans that he was a cosponsor, and he carried the bill on the floor. SB 393 received a short, amicable hearing in the House Revenue Committee, and passed the House with a single "Nay" vote from Rep. Julie Fahey of Euegene, one of the only legislators who did not have a constituent who owned property in the district boundaries. While legislators may file vote explanations, Rep. Fahey did not file an explanation.

SB 901 was unceremoniously "killed" by Speaker Kotek. Under the prerogative of the Speaker in retaliation against Senator Bentz for participating in a walkout to prevent the passage of cap-and-trade legislation, the bill was referred to the Joint Committee on Ways & Means. As the budget had been completed and passed, this Committee had stopped meeting and had no responsibility to meet again to discuss bills that had been referred. Legislators were difficult to contact during the Senate Republicans walkout, and the Co-Chairs did not respond when contacted about hearing requests.

Governor Kate Brown signed SB 394 on June 6 and SB 393 on July 15. Neither bill had an emergency clause, which would have allowed the bills to go into effect on passage. Oregon Constitution Article IV Section 28 says, "No act shall take effect, until ninety days from the end of the session at which the same shall have been passed, except in case of emergency; which emergency shall be declared in the preamble, or in the body of the law." Despite these restrictions, many bills that would not be described as addressing an emergency are passed with emergency clauses.

Both bills went into effect on January 1, 2020. SB 394 was especially prescient, as it authorized the translator district to create an over-the-air and streaming TV station that local governments used to hold public meetings and distribute information during the COVID-19 pandemic. Sinclair Broadcast Group specifically created a subchannel of the Portland Univision Affiliate, KUNP, to broadcast the translator district channel over the air in northeast Oregon and the Willamette Valley while a state of emergency was in effect. The channel broadcast legislative hearings along with a special Zoom call celebrating the accomplishments of retiring State Representatives. After SB 393 went into effect in 2020, a resident of a city surrounded by a translator district who paid the service charge was appointed to the board, finally enfranchising all of the district's customers with representation.

Epilogue: Leading in Oregon

History is shaped by the actions of everyday people living their lives, serving as individuals and as a collective. I encourage every Oregonian to step up and lead in their communities. This may be serving on a local nonprofit board or a city commission, and maybe even running for office yourself. Across my 10 years in Oregon, I have worked to make a difference in the lives of my neighbors through volunteer and civil service, advocating for policies, passing laws, and supporting community leaders without ever having once been elected to a government office. Here are some steps everyone can take to make the Beaver State a better place.

1. Attend local government meetings. Elected governing bodies make decisions based on the needs of their community, which becomes clearer when citizens address them at public meetings.

2. Ask your local governments about public service opportunities. This may be as simple as volunteering at local park cleanups, or sitting on a special district committee.

3. Talk to your local nonprofits and see if they need help. Nonprofits often need volunteers to provide services, fundraise, and lead their organizations on a board of directors.

4. Make public statements, either in the press or on social media. Submitting letters to the editor and posting online allows issues to be addressed more publicly, building public momentum to drive local governments actions

5. Run for office. In Oregon, residents can run for a variety of local, state, and federal offices. Candidates running for water district board must follow the same rules as candidates running for Governor - but not just in the legal sense. Campaigning for local government can often be done using the same strategies as running for Governor.

Making Your Decision

There are usually two really good reasons to run for office: you have some specific policy goals you wish to see enacted by your local government, or you believe that you have a professional background that will allow you to exercise your skills when faithfully conducting the people's business. Maybe you want your local school board to restore funding for a defunded high school music program, and the incumbents have opposed this spending proposal. Perhaps you have just retired from a long career in the private sector and want to apply your business management skills to improving operations at a special district with a poor service delivery record. It is imperative not to run, however, if you just want to become famous or seek to use the office as a quick stepping stone. Planning to run for state legislature two years into a term on a fire district board leaves your local position vacant and burdens the remaining board members with filling the vacancy.

Registering Your Candidacy

Every local government has their own rules for filing to run for elected seats. If you want to run for your local city council, the City Recorder is often the official who will guide you through the paperwork process. If the City is slow to respond, your County Clerk, another elected official, will likely be able to point you in the right direction.

Registering Your Political Action Committee (PAC)

Any candidate who raises, expects to raise, or spends over $750 must register a political action committee with the Oregon Secretary of State through the online portal ORESTAR. Registering a PAC requires an individual to establish a campaign bank account after receiving an Employer Identification Number from the Internal Revenue Service. Each PAC needs their own Treasurer, which may be the candidate themselves or someone else. The PAC may also have several "directors" listed, but this is not necessary. Even if you spend less than $750, you may still file a PAC with the Secretary of State, and publicly posting your expenditures and donations on this website will help you be transparent with voters.

Meeting With Other Officials and Candidates

It is important to understand the issues facing the board or council on which you hope to serve, which can often be accomplished by meeting with incumbent elected officials or the agency's manager. Meeting with other candidates can help you identify common policy goals and lead to future cooperation. If there are four open seats on a seven-member board, four candidates with a common platform can pitch their suitability to voters by pledging four votes to enact those policies if they are all elected.

Receiving Endorsements

A candidate may be well-known in their community or relatively unknown. Endorsements from incumbents or other elected officials can offer your campaign a powerful boost of legitimacy, especially if you are not already a public figure.

Talking to Voters

Campaigns are won on the balance of personal connections that candidates have with voters. Once you have a platform and endorsements from political and community leaders, you need to get your message out to voters. Canvassing neighborhoods, IE going door to door and talking with voters, is the most effective way to win elections. Phone calls rank second, while general advertising in print, broadcast, and digital media are also important. The most important part of political advertising is inviting voters to connect with you, and providing an easy way to contact your campaign or meet with you in person. It will be imperative for you to maintain a digital presence to connect with voters, especially on Facebook. A website will be helpful providing more in-depth information than a social media post or video, and other social media platforms such as Twitter and Instagram may be more helpful in reaching out to younger and more urban voters.

Receiving Endorsements

A candidate may be well-known in their community or relatively unknown. Endorsements from incumbents or other elected officials can offer your campaign a powerful boost of legitimacy, especially if you are not already a public figure.

Talking to Voters

Campaigns are won on the balance of personal connections that candidates have with voters. Once you have a platform and endorsements from political and community leaders, you need to get your message out to voters. Canvassing neighborhoods, IE going door to door and talking with voters, is the most effective way to win elections. Phone calls rank second, while general advertising in print, broadcast, and digital media are also important. The most important part of political advertising is inviting voters to connect with you, and providing an easy way to contact your campaign or meet with you in person. It will be imperative for you to maintain a digital presence to connect with voters, especially on Facebook. A website will be helpful providing more in-depth information than a social media post or video, and other social media platforms such as Twitter and Instagram may be more helpful in reaching out to younger and more urban voters.

Engaging with Political Parties

Few local offices in Oregon are partisan, which means that the candidate's party affiliation is noted on the ballot, and they are nominated by party members in a primary. Most local government offices are nonpartisan, which means that the party is not listed on the ballot.

Political parties usually possess voter data including phone numbers and addresses that can be used to contact voters, funds that can help you purchase supplies and advertisements, and connections with a base of volunteers eager to help your campaign and agenda succeed during and after the election. They also usually have good relationships with elected partisan officials registered with that party, and they may convince them to endorse your campaign or at least meet with you to offer advice. Voter data may also be purchased to an extent, but the information that parties possess will be far more expansive than what your County Clerk can provide.

    Holding elected office can be a very rewarding and fulfilling act of service. Many local governments in Oregon, especially special districts, struggle to maintain a full board of directors and would love to have additional community engagement. Even if you do not win your election, a campaign can open up your eyes to new service possibilities and even spur a government agency to adopt your policy proposals. If you are ready for an expanded public service commitment or have some policy goals you would like a local government to adopt, file at the next election cycle and see what happens.

    Benjamin Franklin told a passerby of the Constitutional Convention that the body was giving Americans, "a republic, if you can keep it," and serving in local elected office ensures that everyday Oregonians keep that republic in place to make a better Beaver State for all of us.

www.ingramcontent.com/pod-product-compliance
Lightning Source LLC
Chambersburg PA
CBHW071121160426
43196CB00013B/2656